The CELTIC COLLE

for Endless Fae & Fantasy Art I

This book is a carefully curated collection of inspiring Celtic, Fairy, and Fantasy-themed images created specifically for members of our Celtic Collective Art Club.

If you're not a member but are simply a fan of all things Fae and fantasy like us, we welcome you with open arms and hope you find endless inspiration here too!

For more information about our Art Club and Podcast visit us at 1scot1not.com

LET'S ENTER THE WORLD OF THE FAE....

Are you feeling a little bit trepidatious? As you should!
Everyone knows you should be VERY careful when it comes to Fairies!

About this Book

As artists and as teachers, we have carefully chosen these images to inspire many of the drawing and watercolor lessons we will be teaching you!
To be clear, using a photo for inspiration doesn't mean copying it.

It does mean:
Taking an idea and **making it your own**.
Learning cool places to put highlights and shadows on your faces.
Taking elements that you see and incorporating them into your own works in **new and interesting ways**.
A **springboard for your imagination** so you can do a completely different version, one that is UNIQUE and special, **and yours**.
Helping you **better understand** anatomy, expression, and poses.
Igniting your creative spirit into taking action to the point where you find yourself RUNNING to your easel BURSTING with excitement to create!

Not sure how? That's what the Celtic Collective will teach you!
We truly hope you're looking forward to this as much as we are!

THE SEELIE COURT
The Friendly Fae

The Seelie Court is the good court, the friendly court of Faeries. Think elves, helpful brownies, little pixies and adorable sprites. Let's think about what we can include in our good Fae paintings and drawings!

We will be creating a lot of gorgeous faces in the
Celtic Collective.
Use the following pages to help inspire and inform
you of those special Fae facial features!

FACIAL FEATURES

The Seelie Faeries will often be beautiful with delicate and/or unusual features (they are Fae afterall). Think about elongating noses, pointing the pixie ears, and creating well-defined and high cheekbones.

The ears are quite magical in and of themselves! Use these references to help inform proper placement, angles and lengths!

Note how the hair falls in front of and behind the ear.

Do all fairies have pointy ears?

Use Karen's Profile Cheatsheet to help you build a perfect fairy profile... from scratch!

Or grab her *How to Draw and Find your Style Book* for step-by-step instructions.

Think of how the facial features change according to the angle of the face.

When drawing and painting faces, experiment with different skin tones and feature placements.

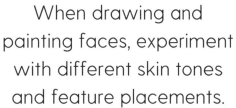

And experiment with various head tilts too!

Lucy and Karen will have lots of lessons to help you learn these skills!

It's not easy but we can do it! Together!

Make up and other facial accessories are also VERY fun to draw and paint.

Use these references to help inform shadows and highlights on your faces too.

Not sure where to put shading or highlights?

Don't worry!

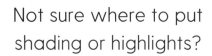

We will show you exactly how to do it and how to use these references to help!

Be sure to take a moment to think about adding details to your pieces.

Where would it be fun/beautiful/ meaningful/cool to add small touches?

THIS is the land of the Fae.

Be creative as you WISH!

MALE FAE

In folklore, the overwhelming majority of real Fairy sightings are of male subjects, we would be remiss if we did not also include them here!

When using photos as references, don't forget we can take any image and make it our own when drawing!

So we can technically use ANY male reference and add on some Fae ears and presto!

Fairy man.

Or use clothing in a clever way so that you don't have to draw the ears at all, and leave the world wondering...

is he even Fae?

Hmmmmm....

I wonder.....

By combining different (or more than one) element(s) in your art pieces, your work begins to tell a story...

Is he a magician?

Or something more sinister...

What if the wolf here was a hare instead?

And the ravens were butterflies.

Suddenly the narrative changes, without saying a word...

CHILDREN

Their faces are rounder and wider than the longer oval shape that makes up adult faces.

Don't forget to use lots of different references to make your artwork piece *truly* your own. Use the position of the girl, but change her wings to those of a butterfly!

Change her crown from flowers to leaves...

Her mushroom top from brown to red and spotted!

POSES

Always use a reference to help you draw a full figure, in any position!

Otherwise, how will you ever know where to go?

The Faerie King and Queen

Incorporate elements of the weather into your artwork! It helps tell the story, set the scene and inspire the artist and viewer alike!

Picking references that have lots of contrast (meaning areas of dark shadows as well as bright highlighted sections) make for artwork that has lots of dimension, depth and DRAMA!

It's also helpful to view your subject in black and white so you can better perceive those areas of shadow and light.

Whenever possible, print your reference images out in color AND in black in white to help you get a concrete understand of value.

WINGS

Fairy wings can be made from anything! Butterfly or dragonfly,
leaves, or even feathers of a bird! We can take inspiration from
so many things when painting and drawing.

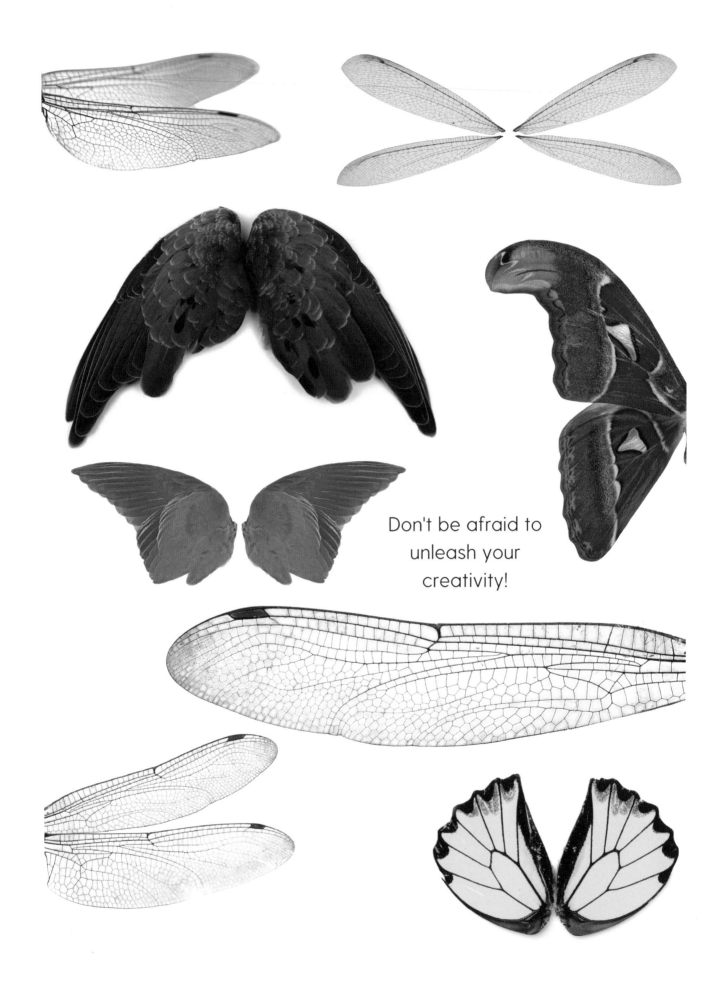

Don't be afraid to unleash your creativity!

CROWNS

Fairy crowns could be made from anything found in nature. From leaves, flowers, and twigs, to seashells, antlers, and feathers!

Spiky, pokey, feathery, smooth or glittery. It's all possible!

Make them as simple or
as ornate as you like!

Use shiny or matte
metal and sparkling
jewels if you're looking
to create a more
medieval or majestic
style crown.

And make
them as
dangly and
sparkly as
you want
too!

Combine all the elements for
even MORE drama!

Fae Clothing

Fairies clothing can be made up of natural materials like flower petals, wool, and linen.

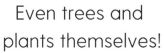

Even trees and plants themselves!

Shoes and boots are made of soft leather tied with strings or even leaves wound round the ankles and calves.

You can depict clothing in your artwork as simply brown swathes of color. Careful use of shading will then help create the illusion of folded fabric. Our classes will show you how!

That being said, always feel free to be creative and ornate as you like when drawing fairies!

Who's to say you're wrong?

Not us!
We love it ALL!

USING FLORA AS CLOTHING

Think how you could use flower petals or leaves to construct fairy clothing.

Or use the floral leaves themselves to create a face or Fae spirit!

Medieval Clothing

Now let's change perspective and consider the
human side of things.
Do not worry, these outfits are just as fun!

Or maybe even more!
Look at those ruffles!!!

All the details and careful,
feminine cut of cloth are
what make these so special
and so very beautiful!

Necklaces,
crowns, belts,
jewels, ribbons,
strings and lace!

Add as many as
you like to your
artwork!

Note the layering of the cloak over the dress. Cloaks are an easy way to dress up your characters and a great excuse to hide hands so you don't have to draw them! Go ahead and gift yourself that gift! It's not cheating, it's just being smart ;)

Similarly, you can draw a headscarf to avoid having to draw difficult hair. Or add horns to the head like this girl, if you're feeling extra crazy!

WEAPONRY

What's sexier than a powerful
woman wielding a powerful
sword?

Not one thing.

INSTRUMENTS

Fairies have been associated with the sound of music as long as there have been sightings of them!

Often times people hear fairy music, even when the fairies themselves cannot be seen.

Unseelie Court
The Dark Fae

Unseelie Faeries are wicked, scheming, and deadly. They like to trick, steal and kill humans and have a particular fondness for babies and young wives!

Heavy use of black in your artwork is a quick, clear and easy way to convey evil.

Pair that with warm tones like orange and red and your dark mood is boldly understood.

Fairies in the Unseelie court are also particularly dangerous as many are avid shape-shifters.

These creatures excel at disguising themselves as handsome men and beautiful women with every intention of luring you to your slow and painful death.

Okay this page is legit starting to freak me out....hehehe!!!

When drawing evil characters, pay close attention to what's happening with the eyes.

A slightly downturned head with piercing eyes looking straight up at you is a VERY terrifying pose!

Or try distorting the pupils. Or adding dramatic make-up! Eyes really are the window to the soul! Especially evil ones!

Make sure you try to capture some of that when and if your artwork calls for some evil!

GOBLINS

Obviously, Goblins are not the most attractive members of the Fae community.

However, there are LOTS of these critters in Fairy and Folklore so it is definitely something we'll want references for when the time comes to create one in our artwork!

GARGOYLES

While also unattractive, adding gargoyles to your castles drawings make for an impressive detail!

Or make up your own freaky gargoyle from a human/animal reference.

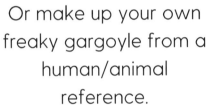

Then use this page to help you figure out how to render your creature to look like it's made out of stone.

Animals

Dark Fae often have animal body parts or features. "Mashing" together animal and human references to make new creatures makes for a truly fun and magical exercise!

Here's a fun example of this:

Claws and Hooves

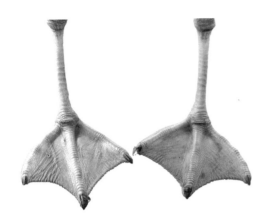

It is quite common for human-looking members of the Unseelie court to have hooved feet.

Yikes! Creepy!

It is also the sign of the devil!

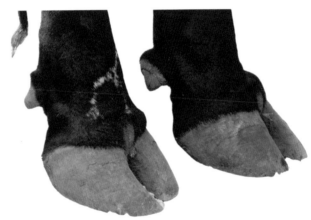

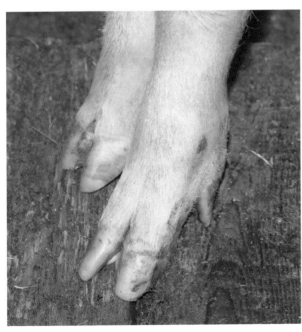

RAVENS

Ravens have long been associated with omens and magic, death, and more.

Try Googling the symbolism of different animals and add ones that have special meanings to you into your artwork!

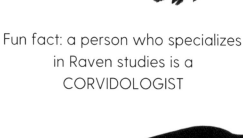

Adding animals into your artwork helps to tell or further develop a story.

Fun fact: a person who specializes in Raven studies is a CORVIDOLOGIST

OWLS

Owl symbolism includes wisdom,
intuition, and supernatural power.

Owls would make a perfect
addition to a Fantasy artwork
masterpiece.

Hares

Are known for their magical shapeshifting ability.

Familiars

All potent witches connect with special animals that help them to do their bidding.

How do you tell the difference between a pet and a familiar?

That is a question only Magick can answer.

Think of different ways you can incorporate animals into your artwork.

And into the lives of your characters.

ANCIENT APOTHECARY

Herbs, Fungi, Potions, Flora, Crystals & More!

In Celtic culture the Faerie world and witchcraft are strongly connected. And what witch would be without potions, magical herbs, crystals and ancient spellbooks! Think about the details you can put in your Fae paintings to add to their mystery.

There is always a
fine line between
witch and
medicine woman
in the middle and
dark ages.

Bottles and herbs,
magic potions
and more
are all so fun to
create!

FUNGI

Magical mushrooms go hand in hand with the Faerie realm. They can make an excellent seat on which to sit on and play the flute perhaps!

They also make background details to add in amongst other plants and flowers!

FORESTS

Use these images to help inspire you to create a dark, moody and magical background!

Think about how we can recreate these effects with watercolors or inks.

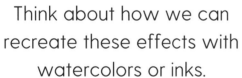

TREES

Fairy lore is FILLED with the magic of plants and trees. The ones here all have significant powers.

Hawthorn

Ash

Rowan

Fiddleheads

Oak

Mistletoe

FLOWERS

Belladonna

There are a plethora of magical flowers!

A great resource to learn more is the book *Scottish Herbs and Fairy Lore* by Ellen Hopman

Foxglove

We will also be studying, drawing, and painting them in the lessons in the Celtic Collective!

Vervain

Foxglove is known as the Fairy Flower as it is though to come directly from the Fairy Realm!

Lily of the Valley

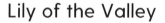

Coneflower

HERBS

Think of all these magical plants as
accessories to your artwork.
Get creative with how you use them!

As a crown...

In the background...

Or a bouquet...

CRYSTALS

Watercolors are fabulous at creating crystals! We will teach you how to paint them step-by-step and incorporate them into your pieces.

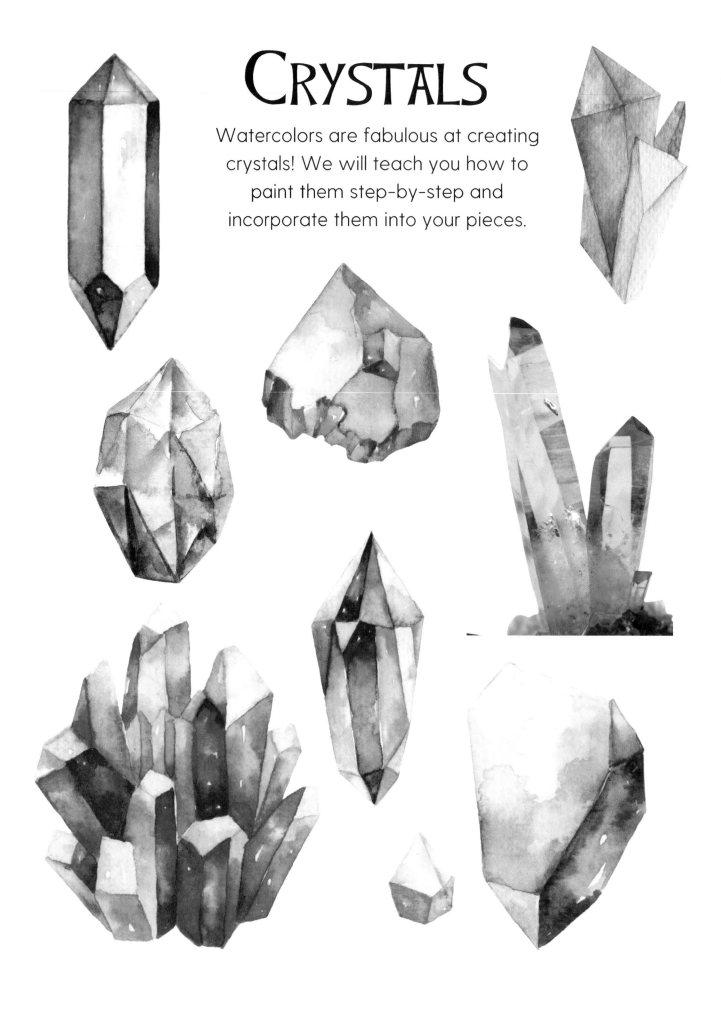

MANSES

Castles, mansions, wee fairy houses & MORE!

Some fairies (like the Redcaps) inhabit old castles, making them scary places. Others (like the Finfolk) build their own underwater palaces! You can also find the Fae in miniature houses built from nature (think tree stumps and toadstools!).

Let's think about what kind of house elements you could put into your paintings! Perhaps it's a wee dwelling off in the corner of your painting.

Or maybe it's the inside of a house so you have to create furniture too! Whatever you decide, we hope these next pages inspire you to get creative and get GOING!

WOODLAND DWELLINGS

Note the details in these images. Notice what's happening in the background and foreground. Notice the stonework and how the light shines through the trees. How can you re-create these in your own pieces in a new or different way?

Notice how wonky all the wee houses are. Keep that in mind when drawing your own fairy houses!

Faerie Mounds & Rings

Sometimes Fairies live in mounds or knolls.

Think about how you can feature one of those in the background of your larger paintings.

Getting to the Fairy Realm is easy if you spot a Fairy Ring!

But be forewarned!!! For ten minutes in the Otherworld can mean years to humans!

Isn't this (above) photo from the Isle of Skye just breathtaking?!

Wee Toadstools

This one is just begging for
a Fairy door!

Can you see it?

Fairy Doors

The Fae can often be seen dwelling amongst tree stumps or plant forms. Think about the cute doors, steps and lanterns you can put in your drawings and paintings to give them a cute place to stay!

CASTLES

Castles don't need an introduction.
They simply are. AMAZING.

Sharpen your pencils.
This is happening!

CASTLE RUINS

While some of the Fae may live amongst luxurious castles, others may dwell in the ruins and tumbled down stones found hidden amongst the hills and forests long abandoned by human inhabitants.

Think about your paintings overall composition. Where could you incorporate something like this?

DOORS & WINDOWS

Doors and windows are strong enough to stand alone as their own pieces of work.!

Turrets & Towers

In addition to the outward, overall shapes of the turrets and spires, also look closely at the gorgeous carved stonework and climbing green ivy going up the sides in leafy decoration.

Details big and small are all things you can borrow and then incorporate into your own pieces.

STONE CIRCLES

Standing stones and stone circles are magical places where you may come across some Fae! Or perhaps you'll catch a glimpse of a ghostly Druid or wild Banshee, keening under the light of the full moon!

Now take that inspiration and see if it sparks an idea for your pencil!

Mythical Creatures

Dragons, Mermaids, Unicorns & so many more!

UNICORNS

Unicorns may seem intimidating to draw or paint but remember, their anatomy is simply that of a horse. You can use any horse reference to get you 99% of the way there. Then use these images to inspire you the rest of the magical way!

You can see this unicorn (top right and bottom) are the same, but have been incorporated into two pieces quite differently!

DRAGONS

They're badass.

Definitely draw or
paint at least one
dragon in your life
if you're a fantasy
fan!!

Kelpies

Kelpies are seriously evil creatures! They can take human form (either as an incredibly handsome man or stunningly beautiful (naked) woman) OR appear as an equally gorgeous white or black horse. No matter what form it takes, it wants to kill you, so all you have to remember is RUN!!!

Or in our case, draw :)

SELKIES

In the water, they are seals, but on land, they shed their skin and take on human form.

Folk lore tells stories of female Selkies being coerced into relationships with human men who trick them into staying on dry land by stealing and hiding their sealskin.

What elements can you included in your artwork that would help tell this story?

MERMAIDS

Mermaid's tales are as old as time.
It all starts with a beautiful woman.
Then add a little bit of...

Seashells
Water
Bubbles
Shimmers
Sparkles
Jewels
Seaweed
A moody sea

A darkened sky
A broken heart.

What story does your
artwork tell?

Refer back to this book time and time again to ignite your creativity!

And to help you tell a more powerful, beautiful, art-filled story.

LINKS

Often times there is information that can be found in a click!
Here are some additional websites that may be helpful for what you're looking for!

 1scot1not.com (info on Podcast, Swag & Art Club)

 youtube.com/karencampbellMIXEDMEDIA
youtube.com/karencampbellDRAWS
youtube.comLucyBrydonArt

 facebook.com/groups/awesomeartschool
facebook.com/groups/lucysartlab

 @karencampbellartist
@lucybrydonart

 amazon.com/author/karencampbell (links books)
amazon.com/shop/karencampbellartist (art supplies)

 Podcast (wherever you listen) 1 Scot 1 Not

WE ARE ALL HERE TO SERVE YOU!

We are so grateful to have you at Awesome Art School. If you have questions, we're happy to help! And if we can make your learning experience better, please reach out, we want to hear from you!

Karen Campbell, Artist/Author, Awesome Art School Owner, Director of the Fun Fab Drawing Club & Mixed Media Society Co-Director of the Celtic Collective
karen@awesomeartschool.com
Taking questions about Supplies, Books, Lessons!

Lucy Brydon, Artist, Co-Director of the Celtic Collective
lucybrydonart@gmail.com
Taking questions about Supplies & Lessons within the CC

For Podcast related questions for Karen or Lucy please email
1scot1not@gmail.com

Margo Brush, Magical Team Member (Customer Support)
magicteammember@gmail.com
Taking questions about Clubs, classes, pricing, books, helping students with login and account issues/status and anything else you may need!

Tara Ciliento, Magical Team Member (Customer Support, Facebook Administrator, Patreon liason)
magicalteammember@gmail.com
Taking questions regarding Facebook, Patreon, billing, password reset help, account changes, status, updates & overall student support.

Jeanette Salib, Artist, Magical Team Member (Customer Support, Facebook Administrator, Resident Artist at Awesome Art School).
awesomeartschool@gmail.com
Taking questions about Facebook, art supplies, and anything happening over on Awesome Art School.

Celtic Collective Members: need log in help? Have questions about posting or issues with your account? Make sure to refer to this GUIDE for all your answers. The eBook is free with your membership!

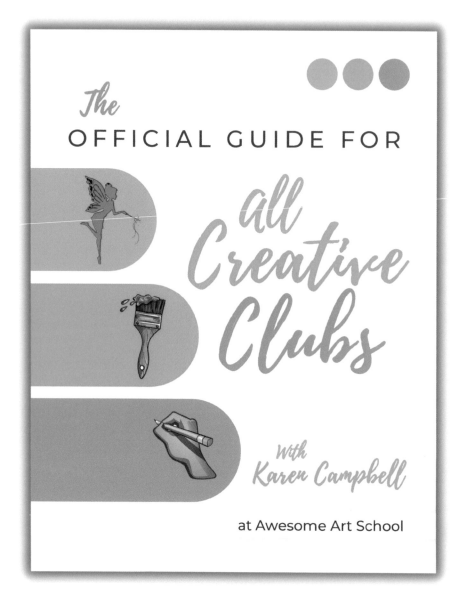

So grateful to have you at...